# POSITIVE
# PSYCH UP

*Supercharging* Your
<u>Purpose</u> and <u>Mindset</u>
for **TRANSITION** Success

PHILIP J. SCHLESINGER

*Disclaimer of Liability or Warranty:* While the author has used his best efforts in preparing and presenting the information in this text, the author makes no representation or warranties concerning the accuracy and completeness of the contents of this book and specifically disclaims any implied warranties of merchantability. Additionally, given all the possible variables involved in a successful transition, the author does not provide any representation, expressed or implied that applying any strategies or opinions included herein will guarantee that a person's sense of purpose will be strengthened, or their mindset will be enhanced, or their transition will be successful. Success in orchestrating a transition and sustaining the needed motivation is the sole responsibility of the reader and participant. *POSITIVE PSYCH UP: Supercharging Your Purpose and Mindset for TRANSITION Success,* includes concepts and ideas that can help a person identify and strengthen their sense of purpose and enhance their mindset during a transition period. The strategies and opinions herein may not be suitable for every person, situation, or objective.

*Requests:* Please send your request to LIFE*and*CAREER INCENTIVES, LLC at pjs@lcincentives.com.

*Library of Congress Cataloging-in-Publication Data:*
Names: Schlesinger, Philip J., author.
Title: Positive psych up: supercharging your purpose and mindset for transition success / Philip J. Schlesinger
Identifiers: LCCN 2025903801 / ISBN 979-8-218-62509-2 (paperback) / ISBN 979-8-218-70066-9 (ePub)
Subjects: Transitions. / Positive psychology. / Career development. / Job satisfaction. / Goals. / Motivation.

"We, like the sun, have the power to forge our own destiny, even when the clouds around us suggest otherwise. The key to our own beautiful sunrise is the <u>VISION</u> we choose to see and the <u>EFFORT</u> we put into the journey."

*Philip J. Schlesinger*

# PREFACE

As much as we all hope that things will go exactly the way we plan or dream during a transition, the fact is that this is not always the case for most of us. Regardless of our level of intelligence, abilities, determination, and hard work, sometimes we lose our sense of purpose and positive mindset, especially during the initial period of a transition as we strive to get our arms around all that is required. When you add occasional setbacks, higher than expected learning curve, miscommunication or inadequate instructions, and the feeling of being overwhelmed by the demands of the transition—along with inevitable unknowns and typical life challenges that sometimes bleed into the transition—a good and healthy *"POSITIVE PSYCH UP"* can make all the difference during the transition period.

Given this ongoing human reality, it makes perfect sense to step back and consider how to weather the transition best (whether expected to be bumpy, mild, or unknown), generate a workable game plan, and execute it to the best of our abilities. *POSITIVE PSYCH UP: Supercharging Your Purpose and Mindset for TRANSITION Success*, was prepared to help in this endeavor.

When we use the term transition, we are referring to both life and career related events which can cover a whole spectrum of changes. Life changes may involve marital status, birth of a child, relocation, college, disability, or other temporary or permanent life changing realities. Career may involve a change in job or career, joining or rejoining the workforce, starting a business, returning from military service, retirement, or dealing with unemployment.

## Transition Strategy

This journey aims to implement the concepts presented herein and capture the perceived benefits of a *"POSITIVE PSYCH UP"* and be the catalyst for a successful transition.

The focus of this book is to help facilitate the supercharging of one's sense of purpose and mindset and add motivation and support during the transition, which can increase the probability of success during the designated transition period and beyond.

What you should expect during this journey is a presentation of a unique and fun platform to help launch and undergo supercharging during the transition period. The supercharging and transition goal support information helps to catalyze positive momentum in your life or career change.

As a note of clarification, the concept of supercharging is not just a fancy word being used but a perceived human response to the application of some powerful psychological concepts. In the context of this book, supercharging will be defined as a **robust boosting and enabling with enhanced vision and passion**.

In a way, there is a striking systemic similarity between the psychological supercharging and the mechanical supercharging. One way a hotrodder can transform a standard motor into an extreme machine is by installing a **positive displacement supercharger**. A supercharger is a forced induction system installed in an engine, comprised of a few critical moving parts, including a pulley, gear, and compressor fan powered by the engine. It pushes compressed air into the engine, allowing for additional oxygen to produce a robust boost of power. The positive displacement engineering built into the process delivers a constant flow of extra boosting power at all engine speeds, thereby better maximizing the full potential of the engine regardless of the RPMs it is turning.[1]

Similarly, from a psychological perspective, we can generate an ongoing boost in purpose, mindset, motivation, and goal empowerment just by implementing a few powerful principles into our daily routines. Thus, by continuous repetition, we can transform them into ongoing, highly effective, positive habits.

As you move forward on this journey, keep an open mind and allow yourself to give *POSITIVE PSYCH UP: Supercharging Your Purpose and Mindset for TRANSITION Success*, a thorough read, and careful consideration. Everyone is different in the way they perceive and respond to new information, but it is essential to be open and go with the flow of the text as you move forward.

As a final note, if your interest is piqued and you cultivate a desire to expand your knowledge of positive psychology, you will likely find the positive psychology-related books listed in Appendix E helpful and worth your time exploring.

# ACKNOWLEDGMENT

I would like to take the opportunity to express my thanks to those individuals and the appropriate representative organizations who were responsive to my request for permission to share their knowledge and insight, which has become part of this project. I appreciate the dedication, gifts, and skill set of all the authors and practitioners who have helped cultivate my interest, knowledge, and understanding of the merits of positive psychology and its practical application to life and career transitions. I also want to acknowledge those who have shared their talents and skills by helping with editing and proofreading and providing kind and helpful feedback.

# CONTENT

# CONTENT

# PART I
# POSITIVE PSYCH UP OVERVIEW

# INTRODUCTION

*POSITIVE PSYCH UP: Supercharging Your Purpose and Mindset for TRANSITION Success*, is both a text and a workbook designed for use during a life or career transition and beyond. This book has three overarching objectives in theory and practice:

1. To help strengthen a person's sense of purpose.
2. To help enhance a person's mindset through ongoing positivity and motivation.
3. To help build a strong support system during the transition timeframe to enhance a person's ability to accomplish their transition goal.

The concepts presented in this book, along with their practical application during the transition period, serve not only current transition needs but can also be a powerful springboard for ongoing success.

One of the biggest challenges in reading and absorbing any content is trying to remember the information, connect important dots, and successfully apply what is presented in practice. With this in mind, the book aims to avoid overwhelming the reader with an in-depth or exhaustive analysis of various motivation and goal theories and to highlight a small number of important and influential concepts.

The book strategically presents relevant supercharging and transition goal support information as concisely as possible in a streamlined manner. To help make the presentation efficient and engaging, an interactive and progressive format, including relevant thought-provoking questions, exercises, and various assessments, is used.

3

With this approach, you should be able to read, absorb, and connect the relevant dots in a personal way, both intellectually and emotionally, in a relatively short period of time. From there, you can formulate your game plan by applying the information in a way that resonates best with you to achieve the desired goal. It is best to approach this journey with the presumption of both personal adaptation and flexibility.

# Supercharging with CIPAC

A well-defined plan should be at the heart of a strong sense of purpose and any worthwhile endeavor to support the goal and help sustain the needed motivation. To create such a plan, we will be introducing and implementing CIPAC. The framework of CIPAC comprises five supercharging and transition goal support layers and will be the heart of our supercharging efforts. These five layers include:
1. Enhancing **Congruency**.
2. Focusing on the **Incentives** you value most relating to the transition.
3. Applying **Positivity** intervention.
4. Engaging in **Accomplishment Journaling**.
5. Accessing the power of **Collaboration**.

The majority of these CIPAC components are referred to situationally at various times at work and/or at home. The one exception to "normal use" is probably congruency, or the word congruent, unless a person is directly involved in a field where the term is used. We will do a deep drive into all five components both individually and collectively.

To help communicate the significance and power of the layers that are included in CIPAC, they will be referred to as

4

**facilitators** [1] going forward. Please consider the following diagram to ascertain the value of these facilitators.

## CIPAC Supercharging Facilitators

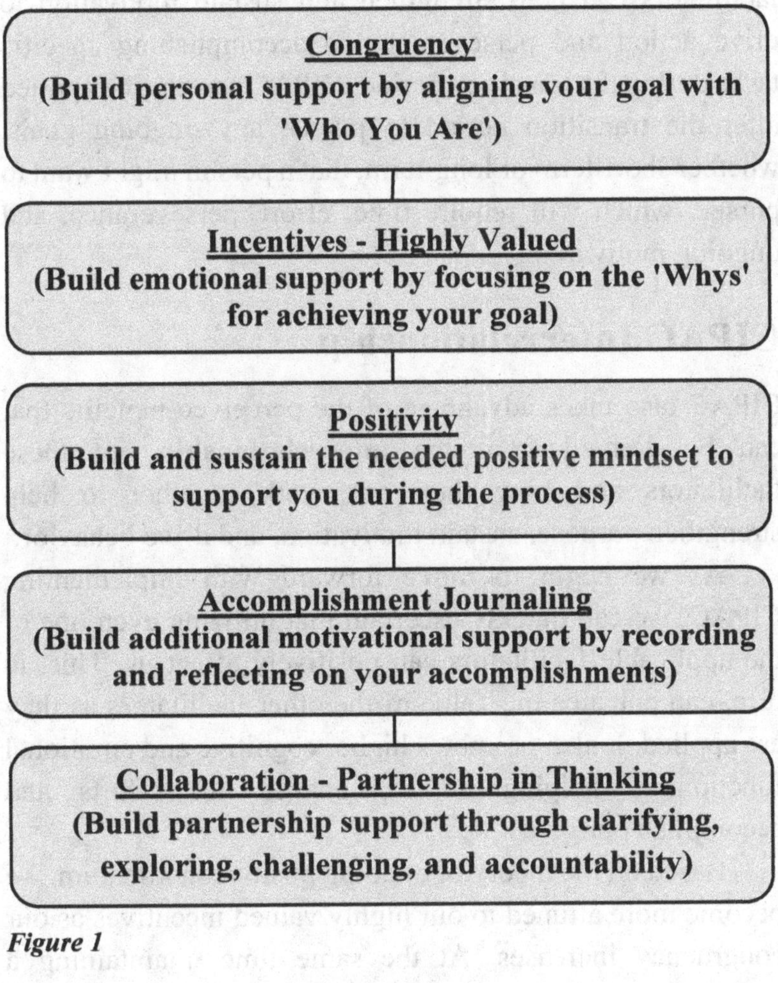

**Congruency**
(Build personal support by aligning your goal with 'Who You Are')

**Incentives - Highly Valued**
(Build emotional support by focusing on the 'Whys' for achieving your goal)

**Positivity**
(Build and sustain the needed positive mindset to support you during the process)

**Accomplishment Journaling**
(Build additional motivational support by recording and reflecting on your accomplishments)

**Collaboration - Partnership in Thinking**
(Build partnership support through clarifying, exploring, challenging, and accountability)

*Figure 1*

---

[1] According to Merriam-Webster, a facilitator is someone or something that facilitates or helps bring about.

5

## CIPAC Premise

CIPAC supercharging and transition goal support are built on the premise that utilizing multiple emotion-based facilitators can help strengthen and sustain motivation to drive action and perseverance in accomplishing specific tasks during the transition period. CIPAC can also be applied after the transition period to pursue any ongoing goals, whether short-term or long-term, that a person might want to pursue, which will require time, effort, perseverance, and ongoing motivation.

## CIPAC Interrelationship

CIPAC also takes advantage of the perceived benefits that can be derived from the **interrelationship**[2] of these facilitators and how they can work together to help strengthen purpose, sustain motivation, and drive behavior.

As we begin to move forward with implementing CIPAC, we can quickly ascertain that utilizing even one of the applicable facilitators can positively affect us. This, in turn, can enhance the value of the other facilitators as they are applied. It also promotes higher cognitive and emotional functioning, helping us supercharge our efforts and accomplish our goals.

Based on the theory of ongoing positive momentum, we become more attuned to our highly valued incentives as our congruency increases. At the same time, maintaining a positive mindset becomes easier. As we focus on our highly

---

[2] How two or more things and/or people <u>connect</u> and <u>affect</u> each other.

valued incentives, our motivation strengthens, reinforcing both our congruence and positivity.

By increasing positivity and minimizing negativity through ongoing interventions, we further enhance congruency and deepen the emotional impact of our valued incentives. Incorporating accomplishment journaling and reflection into this process boosts motivation by making progress visible sustaining our efforts across other facilitators.

Finally, effective collaboration can foster greater personal insight, self-awareness, and perspective, enhancing our ability to maximize the value of all facilitators.

The pictorial below is an attempt to present a high-level visual of the interrelationship of the CIPAC facilitators.

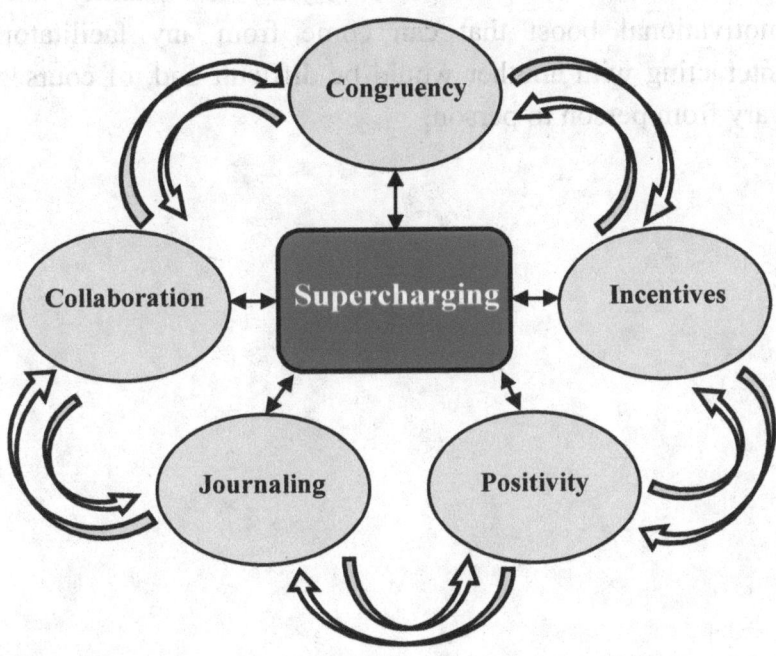

*Figure 2*

Implementing CIPAC into your supercharging efforts is not a one-size-fits-all approach. Therefore, implementing the facilitators is highly customizable and should always be made to fit the person who is implementing them.

Even though all five facilitators are important components of CIPAC, one or more of them may resonate with greater force than the others, depending on the person and how they approach things and based on the circumstances that are involved.

For example, in some cases, there may be a strong sense that our highly valued incentives can produce the greatest bang for the buck in our supercharging efforts. If this is the case, you may want to consider allocating additional time and effort to the incentives facilitator.

It should be noted that trying to quantify the motivational boost that can come from any facilitator interacting with another would be difficult and, of course, vary from person to person.

# IMPLEMENTATION

At first, implementing the CIPAC facilitators into your supercharging and transition journey may seem like a lot of extra effort. However, in reality, it's more of a reallocation of time and effort. It's all about quality and not quantity. It's about creating more efficient supercharging and goal-pursuit habits instead of lengthy, unnecessary task lists.

Since you will be the one who's going to decide how you want to implement the facilitators and to what extent, you have complete control over the effort you want to contribute to the process.

Additionally, because you will likely be highly engaged in the process, any additional effort shouldn't feel too burdensome, especially as you settle into a routine.

## Launch Sequence

The *POSITIVE PSYCH UP: Supercharging Your Purpose and Mindset for TRANSITION Success* journey begins with a deep dive into each of the facilitators included in CIPAC. Each facilitator section is relatively short in content, but you may need to go through them two or three times to fully absorb them.

Following this, you can return and engage in the available exploration exercises associated with each facilitator. Doing the exercises in each facilitator section is meant to be explorative and should involve thorough and careful consideration and reflection.

Following your review, exploration, and addressing the questionnaires and assessments, you can move forward with creating your customized game plan, incorporating the facilitators in a way that resonates with you the most. A fully prepared **Transition Game Plan** example is included for your review starting on page 104. A blank game plan template for use during the transition period is included in Appendix A. A fillable pdf is also available upon request. Request instructions are included in the Summary section of the book.

As mentioned in the preface, after completing your game plan, you would begin the pursuit of your transition goal over the designated timeframe. After completing the journey, you can prepare a write-up of your experience, including what you have learned, felt, and accomplished.

Everyone's situation and desires are different, and a successful transition can mean different things to different people. Therefore, you can structure and utilize your supercharging according to your needs and preference. A few examples may include:

1. Implementing CIPAC into your daily routine as an actual goal for the sole purpose of generating a supercharge and enhancing your well-being during the first few weeks or months of the transition.

2. Utilizing CIPAC for both supercharging your purpose and mindset, and for transition goal support for an important short-term goal that you want to accomplish during the first few weeks or months of the transition.

3. Utilizing CIPAC for both supercharging your purpose and mindset, and for transition goal support for multiple timeframes that are required to accomplish a single longer-term goal.

4. Utilizing CIPAC for both supercharging your purpose and mindset, and for transition goal support for multiple goals that you want to pursue contiguously over the long term.

These are just a few examples of how supercharging with CIPAC can be applied. That being said, the options are unlimited.

# Implementing CIPAC

Implementing CIPAC into your supercharging efforts will include **self-exploration**. It involves taking the time to step back and get reacquainted with yourself to understand yourself better, *"who you are as a human being, and what is important to you."*

It is also important in the implementation process to formulate a clear vision of what you want out of life and career, as well as integrating those things that provide motivation during the transition period to help you move onward and upward—mentally, emotionally, physically, temporally, and spiritually.

To help incorporate CIPAC into your supercharging efforts, the enclosed **Transition Game Plan** was designed to help facilitate the process. The game plan includes the following components and flow:

## 1. Goal (What and When):

Establish the **what** (transition success) by identifying your desired goal and **when** you want to achieve it. Using a goal format such as SMART (Specific, Measurable, Achievable, Realistic/Relevant, and Time based) is a great approach. The primary design of the included game plan template is to identify and focus on a single goal at a time. However, additional template copies can be used for multiple and/or subsequent goals. The primary advantage of limiting yourself to no more than one or two goals during a given transition timeframe is to allow for greater focus on what matters the most.

## 2. Incentives (Why):

Establish the **why** by identifying the incentives you value most and respond to best during the designated timeframe as you pursue your desired transition goal. This may also include various rewards for reaching specific milestones at key points. Incentive exploration begins on page 37.

## 3. Action Items (How):

After establishing the what, when, and why, determine **how** you will achieve it. The **Transition Game Plan** template allows for up to five hows.

## 4. Congruency (Who):

Establishing the **who** by clarifying who you are and what drives you as a human being (e.g., purpose, calling, values, strengths, passions, dreams, etc.). Additionally, compare your "ideal self" against who you are today or what you are currently experiencing. Take note of any obvious gaps. Identify potential incongruences in your thinking and behavior that might prevent you from becoming who you want to be. Also, consider how becoming more congruent can help you see the transition more as a calling or mission rather than just another life or career change.

This can include any aspect of your life, such as relationships, work, home, social interactions, or education. Consider ways to become more congruent. Congruency exploration begins on page 19. There is also a listing of several self-exploration assessment resources that you might find helpful in Appendix D. Please note that they are included as a matter of interest and convenience only and not as an endorsement of any of them.

## 5. *Positivity (Pathway):*

Establishing a positive mindset by engaging in ongoing positive interventions that you believe will help you generate positive thoughts and emotions throughout the time it takes to achieve your transition goal. Positivity exploration begins on page 53.

## 6. *Accomplishment Journaling (Reflection):*

Establishing a habit of recognizing, reflecting, and recording your accomplishments. Journaling can be done anytime during the process and can cover the what, why, and how, as well as anything else about the accomplishment you feel is important to claim and record. Accomplishment journaling exploration begins on page 73.

## 7. *Collaboration (Strategic Brainstorming):*

Establishing the practice of brainstorming with a neutral party and engaging in customized, helpful, and forward moving dialogue. In many cases, this will involve clarifying and exploring your beliefs, opinions, assumptions, perceived or actual obstacles and needed action items relating to the goal instead of what another person thinks you should do. It is about the neutral party engaging in the present moment and nonjudgmental listening and then exploring together. Collaboration exploration begins on page 83.

# Conclusion

In summary, the facilitators included in CIPAC play an important role in supercharging and supporting your life or career transition success.

Enhancing congruency can help fine-tune our efforts by adding additional efficiency based on who we are and how we think. Our highly valued incentives can help generate a supercharge through ongoing motivation and promoting behavior that is driven by focusing our efforts on the underlining whys. Increasing our ongoing positivity can be a desirable springboard to flourish by incorporating positive interventions into our daily routines and mindsets. Accomplishment journaling can work as a natural facilitator of ongoing purpose and motivation that can help push us forward. Collaboration can help open the door to success through greater self-awareness and perspective, as well as a greater capacity to think more strategically in pursuing and accomplishing our goals.

As each of the components of CIPAC is implemented into the supercharging process, it functions as a cohesive and coordinated group. It can help empower us by strengthening our purpose and enhancing our mindset while at the same time feeding our motivation and driving positive behavior to accomplish our transition goal.

As a closing thought regarding implementing CIPAC into your supercharging efforts, please consider three crucial guidelines as you move forward.

1. First, allow your creative juices to flow so the journey can be enjoyable as well as successful.
2. Second, permit yourself to venture out of your comfort zone to visualize better and experience the stretching that comes from effort, perseverance, and accomplishing.
3. Third, and probably the most important, remember to be yourself to maximize who you are throughout the journey without worrying about who you are not. You have to be the best you can be, not the best someone else can be.

With this in mind, let's begin with facilitator number one.

# PART II
# CIPAC FACILITATORS

CIPAC Facilitator #1

# CONGRUENCY

(Build personal support by aligning your
goal with 'Who You Are')

## *Where the 'REAL YOU'*
## *begins!*

# CONGRUENCY

The term "Congruence" was popularized by Carl Rogers (1902-1987) in the field of psychology to describe the alignment between a person's ideal self and their actual experience. According to Rogers, we want to feel, experience, and behave in ways that are consistent with our self-image and reflect what we would like to be, our ideal self. The closer our self-image and ideal self are to each other, the more consistent or congruent we are and the higher our sense of self-worth.[1]

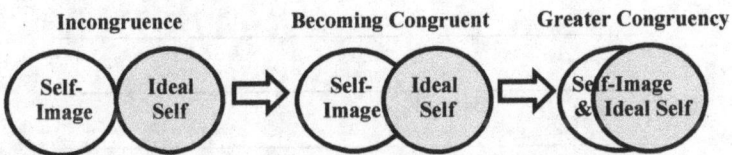

## *Self-Image vs Ideal Self*

1. Describe your Ideal Self (the best version of yourself) in terms of who you would like to be and what you are capable of.

_____

_____

2. What does your current Self-Image (view of yourself) look like? Be kind.

_____

_____

## *Self-Image vs Ideal Self*

3. What are some possible reasons why your current Self-Image is not sufficiently aligned with your Ideal Self?

_____

_____

_____

_____

_____

4. What needs to be changed to allow your current Self-Image and your Ideal Self to be more aligned?

_____

_____

_____

_____

_____

# Additional Clarification on Congruency

When expanding our knowledge base on concepts that are not always consistent with our day-to-day vernacular, drawing from definitional sources that are well connected with the subject is helpful.

According to the American Psychological Association Dictionary of Psychology, congruence is defined as "agreement, harmony, or compatibility, and also a match between psychological attributes and behavior." [2]

On the Congruent Counseling Services website, Mark Donovan (LCPC, LCADC) states that congruence means "a person's thoughts, feelings, and behavior are working together to achieve one's goals." [3]

Given this, it is safe to conclude that living in congruence demonstrates an outward reflection of the inner self while following a desired path or journey.

When we consider whether we are heading in the right direction relating to this facilitator, during any given period of time, we only need to take a quick snapshot of ourselves. If we move towards greater congruency, our daily actions will reflect our values, passions, and strengths and will be consistent with our beliefs, goals, and what is most important to us. If this is our desire, it's essential to know ourselves and, through awareness and effort, ensure our behavior is aligned with our thoughts and feelings.

For exploration purposes, review and complete the additional congruent-related exercises on the following pages. A fillable pdf is also available for these exercises upon request.

## *Identify Your Top Three Values, Strengths, and Passions*

**Values:**

1. _____

2. _____

3. _____

**Strengths:**

1. _____

2. _____

3. _____

**Passions:**

1. _____

2. _____

3. _____


a. In what ways does your life experience currently align and/or not align with your values, strengths, passions, beliefs, and purpose?

_____

_____

_____

_____

## *Values, Strengths, and Passions*

a. Identify three areas of life where your <u>words and behavior</u> usually align with your <u>thoughts and feelings.</u>

1. _____

  _____

2. _____

  _____

3. _____

  _____

b. Identify three areas of life where your <u>words and behavior</u> do **not** currently align with your <u>thoughts and feelings.</u>

1. _____

  _____

2. _____

  _____

3. _____

  _____

## *Identify the Top Ten Things*
## *You Value Most in a Career (or Job)*

Examples may include being creative, applying strengths, inspiring others, pursuing purpose, fulfillment, engagement, opportunity to serve, compensation and benefits, work-life balance, advancement opportunities, challenge, mentoring, positive feedback, etc.

1. _____

2. _____

3. _____

4. _____

5. _____

6. _____

7. _____

8. _____

9. _____

10. _____

## *Values, Strengths and Passions*

a.  In what ways does your current job (or prior job) experience align and/or not align with what you <u>value</u> most in a job and/or future career?

_____

_____

_____

_____

_____

_____

b.  Identify three areas of your current job (or prior job) where <u>your words and behavior</u> usually align with your <u>thoughts and feelings</u>.

1.  _____

    _____

2.  _____

    _____

3.  _____

    _____

## *Values, Strengths and Passions*

Identify three areas of your current job (or prior job) where your <u>words and behavior</u> do **not** usually align with your <u>thoughts and feelings</u>.

1. _____

   _____

   *Primary Reason:* _____

   _____

   _____

2. _____

   _____

   *Primary Reason:* _____

   _____

   _____

3. _____

   _____

   *Primary Reason:* _____

   _____

   _____

# Hints to Develop Greater Congruency

In an article written by Kain Ramsay (international bestselling author and successful entrepreneur in Scotland, United Kingdom), titled ***Practicing Congruence and the Art of Being Real***, he provides some helpful hints in moving toward greater congruency and developing congruent-related habits. He suggests the following:

1. We should pay attention to what we are feeling and thinking.
2. We should be ourselves.
3. Don't hide behind facades.
4. If we are wrong, we should own it.
5. If we don't have an answer to a question, we should admit it.[4]

# Practical Benefits of Congruency

As you might suspect, striving for greater congruency daily can be healthy for us. Moreover, it can provide some measurable benefits in our quest for the desired supercharging and overall well-being. In formulating the concept of CIPAC, which embodies transition goal support, congruency was essential, and it needed to be the first layer and facilitator so that the implementation of the other components of CIPAC could have a natural flow and a seamless integration. There is a strong sense that this facilitator can help open the door to several potential benefits, which can include the following:

1. We can better understand who we are and what we stand for, and where we should be heading.

2. We allow our real selves to come through to see our potential better.
3. We can enhance our peace and minimize the potential for inner conflicts.
4. We can release ourselves from the burden of trying to be someone else.
5. We can move forward in life with a greater sense of purpose.
6. Our confidence increases as we enjoy success based on who we are as a person.
7. We can live each day with greater authenticity.
8. We don't have to hide behind facades.
9. In a nonjudgmental way, we can better accept the need for change.
10. We can open the door to greater personal and professional development as we focus on those values, strengths, and passions that make us who we are.

## Conclusion Relating to Congruency

In a nutshell, congruency exists when our thoughts and feelings align with our words and behavior and are consistent with our values and what is most important to us. It demonstrates that we are true to ourselves regarding who we are and how we conduct our lives. As we become more congruent, we will experience less internal conflict, which can lead to greater peace and harmony.

Given the importance of congruency in our everyday lives, recognizing that we are in a state of incongruence via the disconnection in our thoughts, feelings, words, behavior, and values, as well as a noticeable gap between our ideal self and our current self-image, will help us recognize that things are amiss and need to be addressed. Addressing incongruencies can open the door to real and substantive personal and professional progress. The key to unleashing the power of this facilitator seems to come down to self-awareness and committed follow-up action.

Additionally, relative to our supercharging efforts, it is essential to be aware of what is going on inside (thinking and feeling) and what is going on outside (words and behavior) with respect to our **responsiveness** to the goal that we are targeting and the incentives that are supporting our goal. Consequently, if our goal and the incentives we are using to drive the journey truly resonate and align well with us as human beings (i.e., values, strengths, passions, beliefs, purpose, etc.), they can help ignite and maintain the needed motivation to pursue them with vigor and determination.

## *Congruency Review Questions*

1.  In your own words, how would you best define congruency as presented in the text?

    _____

    _____

    _____

    _____

    _____

    _____

2.  How would you know during any given time that you are congruent, or conversely, how would you know when you are not congruent?

    _____

    _____

    _____

    _____

    _____

    _____

    _____

# *Congruency Review Questions*

3.  What are some of the perceived benefits you can see from striving for a higher level of congruency?

    _____

    _____

    _____

    _____

    _____

    _____

4.  What are some steps you can take to raise your level of congruency during the transition period?

    _____

    _____

    _____

    _____

    _____

    _____

## *Self-Exploration of Congruency*

1. Is your thinking and behavior, relative to life and career, **Congruent**? If not, why not? What needs to change? How will you change it?

   _____

   _____

   _____

   _____

   _____

   _____

2. Does your life and career **Resonate** with you? If not, why not? What needs to change? How will you change it?

   _____

   _____

   _____

   _____

   _____

   _____

## *Self-Exploration of Congruency*

3. Does your life and career facilitate the ability to be **Yourself** most of the time? If not, why not? What needs to change? How will you change it?

_____

_____

_____

_____

_____

_____


4. Does your life and career allow you to use and share your **Strengths** sufficiently? If not, why not? What needs to change? How will you change it?

_____

_____

_____

_____

_____

_____

*Notes*

_____

_____

_____

_____

_____

_____

_____

_____

_____

_____

_____

_____

_____

_____

_____

_____

_____

_____

_____

_____

_____

_____

_____

_____

_____

CIPAC Facilitator #2

# INCENTIVES

(Build emotional support by focusing on the
'Whys' for achieving your goal)

## *Where the 'HIGHER GEAR' is found!*

# INCENTIVES

In its simplest form, an incentive incites or tends to incite someone to action.[1] Generally speaking, incentives come in two forms: extrinsic or intrinsic. The predominant form will vary by person; however, most of us are likely driven by both based on different circumstances.

## *Extrinsic Motivation*

An external incentive to engage in a specific activity with the expectation of a reward or, conversely, to avoid a punishment.[2] Rewards may include money, promotion, recognition, job security, and a college degree. The threat of punishment might involve a possible loss of any of these.

## *Intrinsic Motivation*

An internal incentive to engage in a specific activity that derives from pleasure in the activity itself rather than because of external benefits that might be obtained.[3] Examples may include serving others, creating new things, or the challenge of solving a complex problem.

## Incentive Theory of Motivation

The incentive theory suggests that motivation is fueled mainly by the prospect of an external reward or incentive, which can be either tangible (e.g., money) or intangible (e.g., recognition).[4] Given this, we are more likely to perform a task for the reward rather than the joy of doing the task itself. This theory also suggests we behave in ways that avoid potential or expected adverse consequences. According to the Indeed Career Guide, this theory suggests the following:

1. People are motivated by a "drive" for incentives and reinforcement.
2. Behavior is driven by perceived rewards or the avoidance of punishment.
3. The value of the incentive may change depending on the time or circumstances.
4. People may act differently in similar situations depending on the incentives available.[5]

How this theory plays out in real-time, and to what degree, and for how long, is very much an individual thing, depending on the person and the situation. Maybe the extrinsic and intrinsic are closely related or connected in some situations. For example, can an external reward of seeing a direct report rise to their potential or seeing them master a difficult concept be linked to experiencing the joy of coaching for a manager? Alternatively, can the challenges and difficulties of being a manager, whatever they might be, dampen the joy of coaching and push one more towards the extrinsic or even to the avoidance side of the theory? Additionally, can the extrinsic overlap with true joy?

## *What incentives ignite your motivation?*

_____

_____

_____

# Incentives Drive Human Behavior

On the Farnam Street Media Inc. website, an article titled ***Power of Incentives: The Hidden Forces That Shape Our Behavior*** brings into focus how powerful incentives can be. In the article, the author states that incentives drive human behavior and incentives are the key to understanding people, but conversely, failing to recognize their importance often leads us to make significant errors.[6] In the same article, there is also a reference to a speech by the late billionaire investor Charlie Munger titled ***The Psychology of Human Misjudgment***. Paraphrasing from a small section of the article, Mr. Munger indicated he had underestimated the power of incentives, and every year, his appreciation of the incentive super-power gets pushed a little further.[7]

In today's workplace, companies likewise understand the power of incentives, and they are designing all kinds of individual and team-based incentive programs to help drive greater productivity and boost employee morale. Why are they doing this? It's because they understand the power of incentives and how they influence behavior. Of course, not all incentive programs generate the intended positive effect. There are at least three possible reasons for this conclusion. One, the incentives being offered lack value by some percentage of the targeted group. Two, implementing incentive programs can be poor and/or uninspiring. Third, in many cases, the participants have little or no influence on the selected incentives. Therefore, they may have little or no emotional connection/attachment to the incentives being offered. Despite the various limitations that can exist, highly valued and properly implemented incentives can be effective a very high percentage of the time. Very few things in life

41

appear more powerful than incentives because the underlying focus centers on the **whys**, which typically facilitates our greatest efforts and strongest motivation.

Since you are the one selecting the incentives to help fire up and sustain your supercharging efforts and support your transition goal, and you are implementing this important facilitator into the process based on what is most important to you, it puts you in a great position to harness the power of incentives to help you succeed.

Just for fun, let's engage in a short experiment of curiosity and self-discovery. In the next couple of pages, you will find a quick exercise that involves reviewing and considering a possible intrinsic and extrinsic incentive. This is just a random example with no personal attachment or preference. The purpose behind the experiment is to hopefully generate some deeper thinking about what a highly valued incentive looks and feels like to you and how a certain type of incentive is perceived.

As you proceed with this exercise, notice where your mind and heart go as you read each item and ponder and answer each of the questions to yourself. Upon recognizing where your mind and heart go, consider whether it is consistent with your self-image and ideal self, and what's most important to you, or is it more a result of your present state of mind or circumstances?

# Incentives Exploration Exercise

## *Intrinsic-*

- **LOVE AND PASSION FOR LIFE AND CAREER:**
  a. What does this do for you?
    I. **Feeling the Joy of Fulfilling Your Mission and Purpose**
       1. What does this mean to you?
       2. Why is this important?
       3. How will this benefit you in the short-term, mid-term, and long-term?
    II. **Engagement & Satisfaction**
       1. What does this mean to you?
       2. Why is this important?
       3. How will this benefit you in the short-term, mid-term, and long-term?
    III. **Growth & Experience**
       1. What does this mean to you?
       2. Why is this important?
       3. How will this benefit you in the short-term, mid-term, and long-term?
    IV. **Being in the Position to Help Mentor and Elevate Others**
       1. What does this mean to you?
       2. Why is this important?
       3. How will this benefit you in the short-term, mid-term, and long-term?

## *Extrinsic-*

- **FINANCIAL SUCCESS:**
  a. What does this do for you?
     **I.**   **Desirable Standard of Living**
        1. What does this mean to you?
        2. Why is this important?
        3. How will this benefit you in the short-term, mid-term, and long-term?

     **II.**   **Vacation and Travel**
        1. What does this mean to you?
        2. Why is this important?
        3. How will this benefit you in the short-term, mid-term, and long-term?

     **III.**   **Recognition and Accolades**
        1. What does this mean to you?
        2. Why is this important?
        3. How will this benefit you in the short-term, mid-term, and long-term?

     **IV.**   **Being in the Financial Position to Help Others (intrinsic element)**
        1. What does this mean to you?
        2. Why is this important?
        3. How will this benefit you in the short-term, mid-term, and long-term?

> *__Important Note:__ For purposes of implementing CIPAC, it doesn't matter if a person is driven by extrinsic or intrinsic incentives, or any combination of the two. What matters most is knowing who you are and what you respond to best.*

# Conclusion Relating to Incentives

Incentives are one of the primary sources that fuel motivation and drive behavior to pursue a goal or desired outcome. Consequently, when the perceived value of an incentive is high, and it continues to remain so, the probability of sustaining the needed motivation to pursue a goal will likewise be high. However, incentives can be fickle based on time and circumstances, so monitoring our motivational level periodically is essential to ensure we are moving forward as planned. Suppose our motivation appears to be losing strength. In that case, we should consider finding ways to strengthen the power of our incentives by adding additional meat to the bone or adopting different or additional incentives.

Recognizing the indispensable nature of the right incentives relative to supercharging our purpose and mindset in pursuit of a successful life or career transition is essential. When emotionally connected and attached to the incentives we value most, we find a higher gear and great things can happen. If we rely on incentives that don't align well with who we are as human beings, our motivation can weaken, especially when setbacks or distractions come our way. Incentives can genuinely **support** a targeted goal and can provide the **WHY** behind our desire, commitment, and motivation to achieve the goal regardless of what is going on around us.

## *Incentives Review Questions*

1. How would you differentiate the intrinsic from the extrinsic?

   _____

   _____

   _____

   _____

   _____

   _____

   _____

2. Why are our highly valued incentives such a powerful driving force for action?

   _____

   _____

   _____

   _____

   _____

   _____

   _____

## *Incentives Review Questions*

3. What are some reasons why some incentives are ineffective and don't have the power to sustain our motivation?

_____

_____

_____

_____

_____

4. In your opinion, how do we best maximize the value of incentives to support our transition goal?

_____

_____

_____

_____

_____

## *Self-Exploration of Incentives*

1.  What incentives will be **Important** enough to you to pay the price needed to achieve your goal? Why are they so important to you?

    _____

    _____

    _____

    _____

    _____


2.  How can you best **Customize** your incentives to help maximum their power and sustaining effect during the transition?

    _____

    _____

    _____

    _____

    _____

## *Self-Exploration of Incentives*

3. How and why will your highly valued incentives help you cultivate a **Growth Mindset** during the transition despite possible setbacks and discouragement?

_____

_____

_____

_____

_____

_____

4. How and why will your highly valued incentives help you become **Tenacious** about achieving your goal?

_____

_____

_____

_____

_____

_____

## *Self-Exploration of Incentives*

5. How and why will your highly valued incentives drive **Behavior** to stay committed and locked into achieving your goal?

_____

_____

_____

_____

_____


6. How and why will your highly valued incentives help you create and maintain **Motivation** during the transition?

_____

_____

_____

_____

_____

_____

# *Notes*

_____
_____
_____
_____
_____
_____
_____
_____
_____
_____
_____
_____
_____
_____
_____
_____
_____
_____
_____
_____
_____
_____

CIPAC Facilitator #3

# POSITIVITY

(Build and sustain the needed positive
mindset to support you during the process)

## *Where the*
## *'NEXT POSSIBILITY' is*
## *conceived!*

# POSITIVTY

When we consider the term positivity, it opens our minds to all types of possibilities. However, sometimes it leads us to wonder why some people seem to be blessed with tons of positivity, whereas others struggle to find even a small spark of hope in their lives. As we rub shoulders with folks at both ends of the spectrum, we often become curious as to the how or why behind the person. Life presents plenty of opportunities to experience both the positive and the negative, both personally and professionally.

Even though it seems logical that we are predisposed to having (or not having) a certain level of positivity based on genetics and circumstances, it's just as rational to believe that positivity is a place we can access more frequently when aided by ongoing and effective positive interventions that can help us create positive thoughts and behavior. This shift allows us to enjoy the benefits of experiencing positive emotions more often and more deeply in our lives. This enhances our quality of life and helps us cope more effectively with our challenges and the negative aspects of life.

## Brief Overview of Positive Psychology

In 1998, under the direction of Martin Seligman, then president of the American Psychological Association, the discipline of positive psychology, which emphasizes personal well-being and human strengths, came to the forefront.[1] According to the American Psychological Association, positive psychology is defined as "A field of

55

psychological theory and research that focuses on psychological states (e.g., contentment, joy), individual traits or character strengths (e.g., intimacy, integrity, altruism, wisdom), and social institutions that enhance subjective well-being and make life most worth living."[2]

Since 1998, numerous books and articles have been written, and several studies have been carried out and published on positive psychology. Thanks to the research, insight, knowledge, and contributions of pioneers in this new formalized discipline, our understanding of the value of positive interventions has advanced. These interventions help us move forward in life and experience more of what life has to offer.

One of these early pioneers in the field of positive psychology is Barbara Fredrickson. Her book on positivity happened to be the first one I read on the subject, and I was fascinated by both her insights and the way she presented them. The information and the numerous studies on positive emotions deeply resonated with me and opened my eyes in a powerful way. I first encountered Barbara Fredrickson's work in 2012, during the early stages of a long and difficult personal challenge. Her dedication and contributions to positive psychology have had a profound impact on me.

Her book *Positivity (2009)* suggests that people should aim for a positivity ratio of at least **3-to-1** because this is the tipping point that predicts whether people languish or flourish.[3] Given this, if we can enjoy three heartfelt positive emotions to each negative emotion, we will likely find ourselves on solid ground for flourishing. Additionally, through her research and studies, Fredrickson indicates that raising our positivity ratio helps us build our resiliency.[4]

# Broaden-and-Build Theory

As part of her work on positivity, Fredrickson introduced the broaden-and-build theory. She proposed that unlike negative emotions, which narrow people's ideas about possible actions, positive emotions do the opposite: they broaden people's ideas about possible actions. This increased awareness opens us to a wider range of thoughts and actions.

According to Frederickson, two truths define the broaden-and-build theory that includes the following:

- Positive emotions **open** our hearts and our minds, making us more receptive and more creative.

- Positive emotions **transform** us for the better by opening our hearts and minds, which allows us to discover and build new skills, new ties, new knowledge, and new ways of being.[5]

One way to conceptualize the practical benefits of the broaden-and-build theory of positivity is to ask ourselves how we typically function when we are experiencing positive emotions and are not burdened by the restricting effects that are associated with negativity. I have listed below some benefits that I have personally experienced while in a positive mode. They are consistent with Barbara Fredrickson's research and studies. How does your experience compare?

- Creative juices seem more active.
- More open and willing to learn from others.
- More optimistic about life and the future.
- More graceful in dealing with challenges and setbacks.
- Better able to recognize other possibilities.

- Better able to see things more clearly.
- Maintain a better perspective.
- More patient and tolerant of life's inconveniences.
- Better able to avoid doomsday thinking, and know that setbacks will pass.
- Better able to love and care about others.
- Better able to forgive and forget.

## *Positivity*

What did you experience the last time you had a heartfelt positive emotion?

_____

_____

_____

_____

_____

_____

## Negativity, the Other Side of the Equation

It may be helpful to recognize that negativity is just as powerful as positivity—if not more so—and is certainly more prevalent in society for various reasons. However, negative thoughts and feelings are also a natural part of the human experience and can sometimes be useful. They help us recognize when something is wrong, alert us to internal or external conflict, and even foster greater sensitivity and empathy toward the struggles of others.

Given this, we must ask ourselves whether the negativity we experience is helpful—something we can learn from—or merely a distraction from a positive mindset and personal well-being. If it is helpful, we should seize the opportunity to take action or seek the support needed to move forward. If it is a distraction, we must recognize it for what it is and shift our thinking promptly to rise above it.

## *Negativity*

What did you experience the last time you had a strong negative emotion?

_____

_____

_____

_____

_____

_____

According to Fredrickson, reducing negativity may be the fastest and most efficient way to improve our positivity ratio.[6] Whether by increasing positivity or minimizing negativity, discovering and applying the most appropriate interventions is key to sustaining a higher positivity ratio over time.

## Positive Interventions

Since no two people are the same, positive interventions must be tailored to fit the individual. What works well for one person may have only a marginal effect—or no effect at all—on another. The key is self-awareness and intentional planning, and if necessary, experimenting to refine a personalized approach.

To spark thought and momentum on this topic, I have compiled a list of possible interventions you may find useful. Many of these will likely be familiar to you through your values, upbringing, religious or spiritual affiliations, established habits, and more. Still, it is worth mentioning them, even if only as a reminder. The interventions are not ranked in any particular order and do not represent a complete list.

1. **Maintain an Accomplishment/Success Journal:** Identify three to five things that you accomplish each day, including how and why. Reflect and allow the thoughts and feelings of accomplishment to flow.

2. **Practice Gratitude:** Gratitude can be done in so many ways, such as thanking people when they do something nice for you or even just because you value their love, kindness, and friendship.

3. **Count Your Blessings:** Take the time to recognize your blessings, whether you consider them great or small, and reflect on how and why they are blessing your life. Journaling your blessings is a great way to do the counting and reflecting.

4. **Savoring:** Give yourself the opportunity to savor the good things in life: family, friends, completed projects, workouts, favorite meals and treats, vacations, touchdowns, final grades and awards. Savoring involves enjoying, reflecting, and even reliving the experience the best you can.

5. **Have a Swig of Joy:** Allow yourself the opportunity each day to add something meaningful that helps fill your cup with joy.

6. **Connecting with Others:** Spend time with family and friends. Use free time to develop and strengthen home, work, and social relationships.

7. **Practice Forgiveness:** Allow yourself to forgive and forget as often as possible, especially those things that are petty or insignificant. More substantive offenses may take additional time and effort to release, so be patient with yourself and, if needed, engage in meaningful prayer, meditation (love-kindness), journaling your progress and successes, mental health counseling, or pastoral assistance to help forgiveness come.

8. **Hunt for the Good Stuff:** Make it a practice of looking for the good in people, things, and situations.

9. **Find Ways to Engage in Heartfelt Laughter:** Allow yourself to have a good laugh even if you

need to laugh at yourself for something you said or did. Numerous funny videos on the internet and elsewhere can make us laugh.

10. **Service/Outward Mindset:** Find ways to lighten the burden of other people, and make a journal entry reflecting on the good you did and how you felt about extending yourself to someone else.

11. **Workouts or Physical Exercise:** Push yourself physically and release the feel-good chemicals in the brain.

12. **Blow it and Love It:** Permit yourself to take a $20.00 (or any other amount that makes sense within your budget) and treat yourself periodically to something cool just because you are worth it. Make sure it's not going to make you feel guilty later on.

13. **Focus on Strengths:** Find ways to utilize your strengths more often and more creatively at work, home, social settings, and other activities.

14. **Make Time for a Hobby:** Give yourself time to disconnect and get lost in a hobby.

15. **Take a Stroll Down Memory Lane:** Take time to indulge yourself in your favorite memories that are uplifting and inspiring and bring you joy, such as pictures, videos, journal entries, emails, and clips of sporting events. Relive the experience and the positive emotions.

16. **Success Stories:** Put together a binder of successes that you have obtained in your life, including your degrees, pictures of family, vacations, exercise and sports successes, reaching a challenging person, successful projects, job promotion, blackbelt in

martial arts, a write-up of your extraordinary efforts from a manager or co-workers, valuable learning experience from trial and error, and solving a complex problem. Pull it out periodically to remind yourself of what you are capable of.

17. **Celebrate the Successes of Others:** Cheer for others, and allow yourself to celebrate (sincerely and genuinely) other people's successes.

18. **Enjoy the Beauties of Nature:** Take a nice walk and take in the sights, sounds, and smells of the beautiful earth we live on.

19. **Meaningful Events:** Allow yourself plenty of opportunity to engage in something that is truly meaningful to you.

20. **Inspirational People / Events:** Allow yourself to be inspired by amazing stories of courage, service, and overcoming unbeatable odds.

21. **Engage in Positive Self-Talk:** Accentuate the positive by talking to yourself in positive ways (e.g., compliments, credit, encouragement, etc.) when engaged in goal pursuits, projects, relationships, or challenges. Dispute or counteract the unnecessary negativity.

22. **Imagine the Best Outcome:** Practice seeing yourself where you want to be. Visualize accomplishing each step of the process and not just the finish line.

23. **Positive Affirmations:** Be generous in your positive affirmations to others and yourself. Avoid a robotic approach to affirmations by making sure you establish the basis for the good you are affirming.

**24. Be a Lifelong Learner:** Practice seeing each day as an opportunity to learn and experience new things. This includes practicing a growth mindset, which involves recognizing that you can learn from others, embracing challenges, seeing effort as the key to mastery, trying to learn from criticism, and persisting in the face of setbacks or mistakes.

**25. Expectations:** Practice letting go of unrealistic expectations for yourself and others. Allow other people to be themselves and go at their own pace. Provide others, as well as yourself, with ongoing encouragement and support.

**26. Be More of a Giver Than a Taker:** Practice giving more than you take. Challenge yourself to find more joy in helping others succeed and shine.

**27. Peacemaker Mindset:** Find ways to avoid conflict and division with other people by trying to be more open to differences of opinion and perspective. Whenever possible, focus on commonalities rather than getting hung up on differences.

**28. Use Positive Words More Often:** Practice using positive words in your everyday speech and writing as often as possible. Treat it like a game.

**29. Engage in an Emotionally Moving Activity:** Take time to read, listen, view or engage in some type of activity (prayer, mediation, talent, etc.) that has a positive emotional effect on your soul.

**30. Challenge Yourself on a Regular Basis:** Make a habit of challenging yourself relative to something you wouldn't normally do. Make sure the desired outcome is realistic and worthwhile.

**31. Special Offering:** Find something that means a great deal to you and share it with another person who could truly benefit from it.

## Conclusion Relating to Positivity

Positivity plays an important role in the framework of CIPAC and can significantly increase the probability of success in supercharging your purpose and mindset.

When applying CIPAC, there are two key pathways for incorporating positivity into our supercharging efforts. First, focus on positive interventions directly related to the transition itself. Second, apply positive interventions more broadly to everyday life. Both approaches can enhance our ability to plan and execute our game plan by expanding our thinking, fostering creativity, opening us to greater possibilities, and strengthening our determination and resilience to achieve our goal.

By integrating positive interventions into our daily lives as much as possible, we invite positive emotions to enrich our world and work their magic. However, it's important to recognize that positive emotions can be fleeting due to life's distractions and the tendency for things to lose their impact over time. To counter this, we should treat positive emotions as cherished gifts. Additionally, to sustain their power, we must be creative in our approach—trying new interventions, tweaking existing ones, finding fresh ways to use them, and adopting a rotational strategy. These steps introduce variety and help prevent the overuse or diminishing impact of even the most effective interventions.

It is important to keep the concept of positivity and positive interventions in their proper perspective. There are

65

numerous variables and factors that are continually in motion in both our personal and work lives, and so things may not always go as planned. Given this, patience and ongoing perseverance is an essential element in implementing the positivity facilitator.

Please note that in addition to the normal chapter review questions and self-exploration that follows, there is also a **Positivity Ratio Snapshot (PRS)** exercise that I have created that you might find helpful and fun.

# *Positivity Review Questions*

1.  Based on the text, and your own perspective, how would you best define positivity after reading and pondering the information?

    _____

    _____

    _____

    _____

    _____

2.  Does the concept of striving for a **3-to-1** positivity ratio resonate with you? If so, why? If not, why not?

    _____

    _____

    _____

    _____

    _____

## *Positivity Review Questions*

3. In your own words, how would you best describe Barbara Fredrickson's broaden-and-build theory?

_____

_____

_____

_____

_____

_____

4. Which of the perceived benefits listed in the text, as a result of increasing and maintaining a higher level of positivity, resonate most with you, and why?

_____

_____

_____

_____

_____

_____

## *Self-Exploration of Positivity*

1. During a typical day, is your thinking and speaking more positive than negative? If not, why not? What needs to change? How will you change it?

_____

_____

_____

2. Does your life and career allow you to maintain a **3-to-1** positivity ratio? If not, why not? What needs to change? How will you change it?

_____

_____

_____

3. Based on your current positivity level, does your life and career allow you to thrive as a human being? If not, why not? What needs to change? How will you change it?

_____

_____

_____

69

# Positivity Ratio Snapshot

**Date:_____ Combined Score for Assessment:___ to 1**

*(Instructions included on the following page)*

Q1

5____
4____
3____
2____
1____

Q2

5____
4____
3____
2____
1____

Q3

5____
4____
3____
2____
1____

Q4

5____
4____
3____
2____
1____

# Positivity Ratio Snapshot Instructions

The Positivity Ratio Snapshot is a quick assessment measuring a person's estimated positivity ratio during any given period of time based on any four aspects of life and/or career. You can allocate all four quadrants to a single aspect, four different aspects, or any combination that makes sense to you.

1. Identify aspects that you value most and write them on the line outside of each quadrant. **Life** might include home, school, relationships, self-care, spirituality, financial status, etc. A **Career** might include job duties, success level, job engagement, work-life balance, professional development, etc.

2. Based on your best guess, put an **X** next to the appropriate number in each quadrant that reflects the estimated number of positive emotions you typically have to each negative emotion relating to the specific aspect identified for each quadrant.

3. Add the positive number in each quadrant and then divide the total number by 4. Record the calculated combined positivity ratio above. Are you at or above the **3-to-1** desired positivity ratio?

4. Review the positive interventions included in this chapter, and select your top 10 that you would like to implement during the transition (e.g., 30 days).

5. After implementing your top 10 positivity interventions for the designated timeframe, retake the assessment and compare the two positivity ratio scores. What progress was made? Were the interventions effective?

6. Identify the positive interventions that had the greatest impact that you can utilize going forward.

71

*Notes*

CIPAC Facilitator #4

# ACCOMPLISHMENT JOURNALING

(Build additional motivational support by recording and reflecting on your accomplishments)

## *Where 'ACCOMPLISHMENTS' are claimed and savored!*

# ACCOMPLISHMENT JOURNALING

Journaling is a common practice that serves various purposes, such as recording daily or weekly events for future reference, documenting successes, counting blessings, identifying reasons to be grateful, and expressing thoughts and one's feelings while dealing with challenges or stress. Each of these purposes can be important and bring various benefits to the participant, such as peace, gratitude, confidence, insight, pride, encouragement, and greater overall well-being.

Accomplishment journaling facilitator is an important part of supercharging our purpose and mindset. With respect to <u>accomplishments</u>, there are several enticing and meaningful reasons for journaling them, including:

1. Documenting our accomplishments, whether great or small, communicates advancement and progress, which can become a natural facilitator of motivation.
2. When we recognize, reflect, and record our accomplishments, we open our hearts and minds to what we have actually accomplished, how far we may have come, how resilient we have been (or have become), and what we are truly capable of.
3. Accomplishments (including coping with obstacles or overcoming setbacks) can strengthen our confidence and resilience, which can lead to greater accomplishments.
4. It plants the seed of actively looking for accomplishment opportunities throughout the day to claim and record that otherwise go unnoticed.

5.  It can enhance our overall well-being through the upward-spiraling effect of positive emotions as we take the time to reflect on and savor our accomplishments.

Recognizing, reflecting, and recording our accomplishments shouldn't be limited to tasks and milestones relating to only sizable or significant accomplishments. It is open to any effort and progress you would like to record as an accomplishment. The key is to be consistent and put your heart and mind into it. Now is a perfect opportunity to create the habit of journaling if you are not already doing it.

When making a journal entry relating to accomplishments, it may be helpful to adopt some or all of the following:

1.  Identify three to five accomplishments/successes each day. Also, record what was involved and how you accomplished them.
2.  Record and reflect on how the accomplishments made you feel.
3.  Record and reflect on what you learned and how you can apply those lessons moving forward.
4.  Record and reflect on the why.
    a.  Why did you accomplish it?
    b.  Why was it significant/important to you?
5.  If possible, find a consistent time each day to record your accomplishments. This can make habit-building easier. Perhaps the evening will be the best time to record and reflect on your accomplishments.
6.  In special circumstances or situations, recording accomplishments in real time may help capture the

moment more effectively.

7. Try to note accomplishments in real-time to avoid forgetting them, then expand on them later during your usual journaling session.

8. If you experience discouragement during the day, consider making an accomplishment journal entry in the moment to help counteract the discouragement.

## Conclusion Relating to Journaling

Accomplishment journaling is a powerful facilitator because it can speak loud and clear as to the success we are experiencing and, the things that we are accomplishing and have accomplished. It is both reflective and visual and connects us more deeply at an emotional level to a given success story, from the first step through the desired finish line and beyond. The return on our investment of time in meaningful accomplishment journaling has the potential to pay some very healthy dividends.

Before moving on to the self-exploration exercise for this facilitator, consider the sample accomplishment journal entry on the following page.

## *Accomplishments Journal Entry*

Date *May 17*                What, How, and Why?

### 1. *Morning Workout* –

*I got up this morning at the planned time and did my 45-minute workout. It went well and I pushed myself hard. I love the challenge. Great effort!*

### 2. *Weekly Project Manager Meeting* –

*The creative juices were flowing this morning as I prepared for my meeting. The meeting went great. My manager and co-workers complemented me.*

### 3. *Lunch With Direct Report* –

*I have noticed that Rick has been struggling at work lately so I invited him to lunch. We had a good discussion and afterward he told me that it was really helpful to talk through a specific issue he was dealing with. During the rest of the day, he appeared energic, focused and productive.*

### 4. *Quiet Time* –

*I did my evening scripture study and meditation. I also took a few minutes to reflect on my experience with Rick today. It feels really good to help another person in need. GREAT DAY!!!*

# *Self-Exploration of Accomplishment Journaling*

1. Have you ever engaged in journaling in the past that was specifically focused on accomplishments, including the what, how, and why? If so, how did you feel, and what was your mindset following the experience?

_____

_____

_____

_____

_____

2. Why do you believe that recording and reflecting on our accomplishments has the power to enhance our drive and motivation?

_____

_____

_____

_____

_____

# *Self-Exploration of Accomplishment Journaling*

3. Does your life and career provide you ample opportunity to write and reflect on your accomplishments (small and large)? If not, why not? What needs to change? How will you change it?

_____

_____

_____

_____

_____

_____

_____

_____

_____

_____

_____

_____

_____

_____

_____

# *Notes*

_____
_____
_____
_____
_____
_____
_____
_____
_____
_____
_____
_____
_____
_____
_____
_____
_____
_____
_____
_____
_____

CIPAC Facilitator #5

# COLLABORATION -
# Partnership in Thinking

(Build partnership support through clarifying, exploring, challenging, and accountability)

## *Where 'Aha Moments' surface!*

# COLLABORATION

No doubt, most of us have heard the term, "No man is an island." It is probably safe to say that there are times when collaborating with another person can make all the difference in the world in helping us achieve a desired outcome. Collaboration can take various forms, but the goal here is to specifically focus on the value of collaboration in relation to our own thought processes.

Whether we care to admit it or not, we can all get stuck in our own heads, making it difficult to determine the best way forward. We might be grappling with a difficult question and just can't seem to come up with the right answer, or we have an important decision to make, but the correct path isn't clear. In many cases, this isn't because we lack the ability to figure it out—it's often because the best answer, or the path to it, hasn't been triggered due to restrictive internal dialogue. Sometimes, no matter how hard we try or how long we think about something, the right answer won't surface without another person asking the right questions or challenging our thinking.

There is actually a profession—life coaching—that focuses specifically on helping people work through their own thought processes to arrive at the right answers and solutions. To illustrate the role of the collaboration facilitator, it is useful to examine it through the lens of the life coaching profession. Whether we choose to work with a life coach or prefer to collaborate with a family member, trusted friend, mentor, or boss, understanding collaboration from a life coach's perspective is valuable. After all, collaborative communication (or strategic brainstorming) is at the very core of what they do.

Coaches trained in International Coaching Federation (ICF)–approved programs, incorporating ICF standards and competencies, focus on helping clients expand their thought processes and perspectives through exploration.[1] This helps clients determine the best way forward in reaching their personal or professional goals. It is important to note that life coaching is not a form of mental health counseling, nor is it a consulting or advisory service.

Generally speaking, the objective of life coaching is to assist individuals in pursuing their goals by helping them explore their beliefs, opinions, perceptions, assumptions, passions, obstacles, fears, and other relevant issues. This type of collaborative communication can be highly effective in helping us move forward toward our desired goals.

The fact is, this kind of collaborative communication can be a powerful learning process. No matter how intelligent we may be, we all get stuck in our own thought processes at times, struggling to find needed answers and solutions. Collaboration can help bring these answers to the surface, answers that may already be stirring inside us but have yet to fully emerge.

Effective collaborative communication is built on a non-advisory platform where the other party does not tell us what to do or how to do it. Instead, they listen to the information we provide and, in a nonjudgmental manner, ask clarifying and exploratory questions tailored to our specific situation. Additionally, they share back what they have heard during the discussion giving us the opportunity to hear and process our own words from another's perspective. This will help us confirm whether what we are thinking and communicating truly aligns with our intentions.

In some cases, the other party may determine that it would be helpful to challenge our thought processes—either because they notice inconsistencies in our thinking or because of how we are communicating our ideas. This challenge should stem from careful observation rather than a difference of opinion. Such a check-and-balance system can be instrumental in uncovering potential blind spots or gaps in our thinking. Once we grant permission for their input, it is important to allow them to speak without interruption and see where the discussion leads. While we are not obligated to agree with them, once we invite their perspective, we should be open to hearing it fully. Additionally, while we may occasionally seek suggestions— or the other party may feel strongly about offering them— this should be the exception rather than the rule.

To ensure a successful collaborative experience, two foundational principles must be established and maintained throughout the course of our collaboration efforts.

First, a trusting relationship must exist between us and the other party. Trust opens the door to meaningful dialogue and enables us to share openly. In a collaborative communication setting, we need to trust that the other party will listen attentively, focus on what we share, and ask thought-provoking, forward-moving questions in a nonjudgmental manner. When a trusting, collaborative relationship develops, a safe environment for exploration emerges. Without this safe space, identifying the relevant core issues may be difficult.

Second, we must also do our part in the communication

process. This means not only trusting the other party but also trusting the process itself. Trusting the process requires us to be open, willing to share, and ready to explore new perspectives. Collaborative communication should be viewed as a "*partnership in thinking*." However, if we hold back—whether regarding our thoughts, assumptions, beliefs, goals, or barriers—our progress may be limited. Patience with the process is also essential, as it takes time for relevant insights to surface and connect.

At this point, you might be asking yourself: "Now that I understand collaborative communication better, what's in it for me from a practical standpoint?" In Marcia Reynolds's book *Coach The Person, Not The Problem (2020)*, she outlines several benefits that can be derived from engaging in the thought process through reflective inquiry (reflection and follow-up questions). Some of these benefits include:

- Helping us explore our own thinking when there is uncertainty related to decisions and actions.
- Helping us recognize possible gaps in our logic.
- Helping us clarify our fears and desires.
- Helping us use our creativity and resources to see beyond roadblocks.
- Helping us stop and question the thoughts and behavior that limit our perspective so we can see a new way forward.
- Helping us think more broadly, beyond our fears, inherited beliefs, and assumptions that limit possible actions .[2]

Relative to collaboration, it would be wise to avoid giving up on ourself too quickly by seeking advice from the other party. However, if sufficient time and exploration have not produced the expected results, we can proceed, if we feel strongly about doing so. The primary objective is to integrate the other party into our thought processes through reflective inquiry, allowing us to determine for ourselves the best way forward, whether that aligns with our original thinking or it requires an adjustment based on a shift in our perspective.

As we move forward and engage in collaborative communication, it may be helpful to outline what a typical life coaching session might look like in real time. This can serve as a model for our own collaborative discussions or brainstorming sessions. These sessions generally range from fifteen minutes to an hour and typically consist of three phases: a beginning, a middle, and an end. The three phases may resemble the following:

## *Beginning-*

1. Establish a collaboration discussion agenda at the beginning of a session that includes:
   a. Identify the focus of the session and the goal you want to achieve. Clarify what the goal means to you. Why is the goal important? What are some of the perceived benefits of accomplishing the goal?
   b. Identify and prioritize the issues you want to explore during the session to help you move forward. Issues may include components of the goal, barriers/obstacles to success, action items needed, and whether possible shifts in our thinking or any behavioral changes might be advantageous. Prioritize based on what is most important.

   c. Identify a reasonable measure of success for the session, given the issues being explored, their priority, and the allotted time for the session.

## *Middle-*

1. Engage in a detailed question-and-answer dialogue. Share information about the goal, explore relevant issues, address obstacles/barriers to success, and discuss possible action items.
2. Provide meaningful feedback to the other party regarding their line of questioning to ensure the discussion is helpful to you and moves you forward.
3. The other party may challenge your thought processes, when needed, through observation and follow-up thought-provoking questions (what and how) to help uncover possible blind spots or gaps in your thinking.
4. Exploring emotions that surface during the session may be helpful and desirable.

## *Ending-*

1. Discuss insight gained during the session, including how it impacts you going forward.
2. Discuss progress towards your stated goal, both the session goal and the overall transition goal.
3. Finalize the action items that are needed and your commitment to completing them.
4. Discuss and agree upon accountability measures, and the role each party would play in the process.

5. Reflect and share final thoughts and progress achieved.
6. If applicable, decide on a day and time for the next session.

## Conclusion Relating to Collaboration

Collaborative communication (or strategic brainstorming), which involves clarifying, exploring, challenging, action planning, and accountability, can be one of the best ways to supercharge our efforts and see success.

For the purpose of a recap, here are six important guidelines for collaborative communication that we have addressed and should apply in practice:

1. A trusting relationship between us and the other party is essential to ensure that collaboration remains open and effective.
2. Effective collaborative communication requires us to willingly and openly engage with the other party as we clarify and explore together. We need to trust both the process and the other party.
3. The other party must function as a neutral participant—one who not only cares about our success and remains nonjudgmental but also stays objective and honest, even if it pushes us out of our comfort zone.
4. It is important to remember that the other party should not be seen as a problem solver, nor should they act as our advisor. Their role is to help expand our thought processes through reflective inquiry, allowing us to arrive at the right answers ourselves rather than being told what to do and how to do it.

5. Patience in the process is sometimes required to achieve a successful outcome. Multiple sessions are common because complete answers and expected results don't always emerge in a single session. Additional time may be needed to work through all relevant issues.

6. Accountability and ongoing support are essential to success.

It is very important to remember that the primary objective here is forward movement—helping us get where we want to be. This form of collaboration becomes more efficient with time and practice. Though a checklist may be helpful to the partnership at first to get the ball rolling, the ultimate goal is always present moment listening and exploring based on what we share with the other party.

Please review and complete the exercises on the following pages.

## *Collaboration Review Questions*

1. How would you best define collaborative communication as presented in the text?

_____

_____

_____

_____

_____

_____

2. What are the primary objectives behind collaborative communication?

_____

_____

_____

_____

_____

_____

_____

## *Collaboration Review Questions*

3. What are the two important foundational principles to help ensure effective collaborative communication? Why are they essential?

_____

_____

_____

_____

_____

_____

4. As a general rule, what does effective collaborative communication not involve, and why?

_____

_____

_____

_____

_____

# *Self-Exploration of Collaboration*

1. Have you ever engaged in collaborative communication in the past that was related to a specific goal, including the what and how? If so, what did you learn, and how did it help you move forward?

   _____

   _____

   _____

   _____

   _____

2. Now that you better understand collaborative communication, provide an example of a situation where you could have benefited from this type of collaboration. Why would it have been helpful?

   _____

   _____

   _____

   _____

   _____

## *Self-Exploration of Collaboration*

3. Based on the information that has been presented on collaborative communication, how do you feel it can help provide forward movement?

_____

_____

_____

_____

_____

_____

_____

_____

_____

_____

_____

_____

_____

## *Notes*

_____
_____
_____
_____
_____
_____
_____
_____
_____
_____
_____
_____
_____
_____
_____
_____
_____
_____
_____

# PART III

# CUSTOMIZING YOUR TRANSITION

# TRANSITION GAME PLAN

Before presenting the **Transition Game Plan** template, perhaps it would be helpful to share a few thoughts on designing and executing a game plan.

One of my greatest passions in life is college football. I love the excitement surrounding every new season on the gridiron, and I also experience sadness when the college football season ends after the national championship game. Occasionally, as it relates to my favorite team in my home state of Utah, when they have an off year, I find myself hoping the season ends quickly because I can't take it anymore. Luckily for me (and those around me), this doesn't happen very often. Most seasons, my team does reasonably well, and I'm proud of their accomplishments, especially given the uniqueness of the university and some of the challenges and limitations that the coaches have to navigate through.

On a more micro level, game by game, it is interesting how each game can seem to take on a life of its own for me. Such is the nature of sport. It's almost like I have a preconceived expectation of how the team should perform without a clear understanding of all the facts that will come into play—such as the talent level of the players in comparison to the competition, scouting report of the other team's strengths and weaknesses, injury report, how the week of practice went, offensive and defensive game plans, and the mental and physical preparation of the players.

Despite my lack of knowledge and understanding of all the facts and the possibility that the team could have an off day—I often shake my head, wondering who came up with the game plan. For some reason, the game plan and the coaches always seem to be the first place I go. Why doesn't the offensive coordinator see that trying to run to the left doesn't work? Or why does he call such a dumb play, given the situation or the current flow of the game? Why does the defensive coordinator always seem to wait until halftime to make adjustments that could have been made after the first two series when the other team is already up by two touchdowns? Despite what I think I might know, armchair quarterbacking is not very productive—especially without all the relevant facts.

Perhaps you are wondering where I am going with all this? Well, I would submit that as important as preparation (mental and physical) and execution are to the overall success of an endeavor, generating the right game plan—after compiling and analyzing all the relevant facts—is absolutely essential. Additionally, these three components (game plan, preparation, and execution) need to be aligned, or, as we have covered earlier, they must be congruent.

Having said this, I have a few suggestions related to the formulation and execution of your game plan.

**Number one**, carefully consider the facilitators presented herein and move forward with them in a way that resonates best with you, understanding that patience and flexibility may be required as you navigate the process. Also, because you are uniquely you, the facilitators must be customized specifically to yourself. Despite what others may think, no one on earth really knows you better than yourself; therefore, you will usually know what will work best.

**Number two**, there is no substitute for effort. One of the most important truisms in life is that no matter what journey we choose to travel, the effort we put into it is what really counts. Any accomplishment, great or small, isn't really an accomplishment unless we put forth the relative effort that will allow us to claim it as such. If we do the very best we can under any given set of circumstances, we can always feel good about what we have accomplished—even if we come up a little short.

**Number three**, avoid unnecessary perfectionism. This doesn't mean we shouldn't strive for excellence (or relative perfection) because we are all capable of "striving" for our personal best. Still, the expectation of perfection represents a standard without consideration of or allowance for the human factor—which includes imperfections, setbacks, distractions, occasional off days, and the unexpected.

**Number four**, as much as possible, focus more on the journey itself and let the end result take care of itself.

**Lastly**, control what you can control and let the rest go. Sometimes, this can be a challenge; however, setting a goal that incorporates aspects that are beyond our control can oftentimes lead to frustration and unneeded stress.

In the following pages, there is an example of a fully populated game plan for review. A blank set for your use is included in Appendix A. The game plan example presented represents one of many possible approaches to a new job transition. With this particular transition game plan, the primary goal is centered on integrating all five CIPAC facilitators themselves into one's personal and work life as the catalyst for driving a successful transition rather than any specific goal relating to the new job itself.

Please note that a separate fillable pdf version of the **Transition Game Plan** is also available upon request.

# TRANSITION GAME PLAN

### I. GOAL DETAIL (What, When, Why & How):

### A. <u>WHAT</u> I Want to Accomplish (life or career related, or both):

*Orchestrate a successful new job transition during my first 100 days. A successful transition means learning my job tasks, understanding expectations, gaining the trust of my team members, feeling comfortable with my manager, and developing confidence in my role.*

### B. <u>WHEN</u> I Want to Accomplish My Goal:

**Start Date** *April 1*      **Completion Date** *July 10*

### C. <u>WHY</u> I Want to Accomplish My Goal (Most Valued Incentives):

### 1. Incentives Relating to My Goal -

**Most Valued Incentive #1** *Strong Impression*

***Reason:*** *It will go a long way in setting the tone in my working relationships and development.*

**Most Valued Incentive #2** *Future Promotions*

***Reason:*** *Opportunity for greater income potential.*

**Most Valued Incentive #3** *Confidence Boost*

***Reason:*** *A successful transition will generate a huge boost of confidence for me going forward.*

### 2. Milestone Reward/Recognition (based on specific date, completion percent etc.) -

**Date:** *Apr 30-30%*  **Reward:** *Ruth Chris Steakhouse*
**Date:** *May 30-60%*  **Reward:** *Weekend Getaway*
**Date:** *Jul 10-100%*  **Reward:** *Backpacking Trip - AZ*

# TRANSITION GAME PLAN

**D. HOW I Plan to Accomplish My Goal:**

**How #1 to Accomplish My Goal – by doing what (most important)?**
*Implement the CIPAC facilitators into my daily routine for 100 days. Read game plan every morning.*

**How #2 to Accomplish My Goal – by doing what (second most important)?**
*Daily 45-minute workouts; balanced nutrition plan (60% protein, 30% carb, 10% fat), and seven hours of sleep each night. Journal my accomplishments.*

**How #3 to Accomplish My Goal – by doing what (third most important)?**
*Focus on implementing two or three positive interventions during the day as outlined in Section III of the game plan. Journal my accomplishments.*

**How #4 to Accomplish My Goal – by doing what (fourth most important)?**
*Practice being more congruent as outlined in Section II of the game plan. Journal my accomplishments.*

**How #5 to Accomplish My Goal – by doing what (fifth most important)?**
*Access the power of Collaboration as outlined in Section V of the game plan. Journal each session.*

# TRANSITION GAME PLAN

## II. CONGRUENCY ENHANCEMENTS:
Based on self-exploration, identify three areas of congruency to enhance during the transition.

**Congruency Enhancement #1:** *Align Better With My Values, Strengths And Passions*
*How to Accomplish – by Doing What?*
*Do periodic daily checks to ensure that my thoughts, feelings, and actions are consistent with my values, strengths and passions, and what's most important. Upon detection of incongruence make adjustments. Set a timer every few hours to stay on top of my checks.*

**Congruency Enhancement #2:** *Don't Take Things Personally*
*How to Accomplish – by Doing What?*
*Maintain a clear understanding from day one that feedback from my manager and co-workers is essential to my transition and job success. Be chill and open. Put reminder notes in strategic places.*

**Congruency Enhancement #3:** *Avoid Harmful Perfectionism*
*How to Accomplish – by Doing What?*
*I know that I am imperfect and can make mistakes or fall short, and so I don't need to beat myself up when things don't go perfectly. Be more compassionate with myself, and practice positive self-talk to counteract unnecessary perfectionism. Put reminder notes in strategic places.*

# TRANSITION GAME PLAN

## III. POSITIVITY:
Based on self-exploration, identify ten interventions that can help accentuate the positive during the transition.

| Top Five | Additional Five |
|---|---|
| 1. *Positive Self-Talk* | 1. *Outward Mindset* |
| 2. *Hunt for the Good Stuff* | 2. *Time for a Hobby* |
| 3. *Focus on Strengths* | 3. *Visualize Success* |
| 4. *Count My Blessings* | 4. *Connect More* |
| 5. *Consistent Workouts* | 5. *Pos Affirmations* |

## IV. ACCOMPLISHMENT JOURNALING:
x **Daily**  *Note in real time and journal in the evening.*
**Every Other Day**
**Twice a Week**
**Weekly**

## V. COLLABORATION – Thinking, Support, & Accountability Partners:

| | |
|---|---|
| 1. *Manager* | 4. *Mentor* |
| 2. *Co-Workers* | 5. *Close Friend* |
| 3. *Significant Other* | 6. *Sibling* |

**Commitment:** *One or two 30-minute collaborative session each week to account for the week, discuss progress, and explore issues.*

# PART IV

# SUMMARIZATION

# SUMMARY

Presenting *POSITIVE PSYCH UP: Supercharging Your Purpose and Mindset for TRANSITION Success* has been a real pleasure. I hope that you find success in your efforts to generate the desired supercharge and transition, whatever form it represents. Please remember that the supercharging and transition goal support concepts and ideas presented herein should be viewed as an outline or approach that can be fashioned and applied in any manner that works best for you. Even though the supercharging can facilitate the desired transition period, you are always welcome and encouraged to undergo the supercharging as often as you like, involving any short-term, mid-term, or long-term goal.

As presented in this text, CIPAC is made up of five powerful facilitators designed to drive the supercharging and to help ensure a successful transition.

**Congruency** is about aligning our words and actions with our thoughts and feelings and ensuring they are consistent with our values, strengths and what is most important to us. As we strive for greater congruency, we will see our self-image and our ideal self more consistently aligned and harmonious.

**Incentives** are about focusing our efforts on the whys and what we value most relating to the desired goal, then targeting them to help generate motivation and drive behavior.

**Positivity** is about enhancing our mindset, perspective, and overall well-being through positive interventions to support and sustain us during the supercharging and transition timeframe.

111

**Accomplishment journaling** is about recognizing, recording, and reflecting on our accomplishments, which can help facilitate ongoing motivation throughout the process.

Lastly, **Collaboration** is about engaging in a thinking partnership with a neutral party to freely explore and help bring answers and solutions to the surface, facilitating forward movement. Collaboration can also be helpful in terms of having a supportive ally and an accountability partner.

Concerning the collaboration facilitator, you may also find it helpful to visit the International Coaching Federation (ICF) website at https://coachingfederation.org/ to learn more about professional life coaching and how coaches use the process of collaborative communication to help their clients move forward and thrive.

## Establishing Supercharging Habits

A common belief relating to any established habit (good or bad) is that upon triggering, based on some cue, we seem to subconsciously shift into a predetermined routine that our brain defaults to as a result of a prior neural mapping established around a desired outcome.

Thanks to the blessing of neuroplasticity, we can, to some degree or another, retrain our amazing brain to help modify our behavior.[1] With this ability, we can form new or better positive habits and use them to help generate a desired supercharging. Whether a new or better habit takes twenty-one days to become established, as many believe, or one day or even one year, it doesn't really matter because not all people or habits are the same. The only timeframe that matters for us is the time it takes to seal the deal.

With this in mind, as you experiment with the various components of CIPAC in ways that resonate best with you and experience success utilizing them, would it not be advantageous to consider adopting CIPAC, or some components of CIPAC, in your goal pursuit habits going forward? Of course, its application can be implemented anytime you feel the need to, even when dealing with an unexpected challenge at work, home, or school, or even something minor such as a lingering discouraging thought. We can freely draw upon any aspect of CIPAC, such as a positive intervention (e.g., hunting for the good stuff, exercise, taking a walk, service to others, prayer, meditation, etc.) to help generate a quick boost that will allow us to keep moving forward.

## Reflection Write-up

After completing your supercharging and transition journey (whatever time period you have selected), you can reflect on and document your journey in the next few pages. The reflection write-up should be thorough and descriptive. It should include such things as the benefits derived from utilizing CIPAC to enhance your sense of purpose, mindset and goal pursuits; improvement in your well-being; things you learned about yourself; successes obtained; obstacles you encountered and overcame; confidence gained and/or strengthened; resilience shown; new perspectives gained; and changes in behavior. Given that this is your transition journey, take whatever time is needed to share what has been most impactful for you during your journey, and how you can apply what you have learned going forward.

# Final Note

As previously mentioned in the text, all questionnaires, self-exploration exercises, assessments, reflection write-up, accomplishment journal entry, note sections, and Transition Game Plan, included in the text and the appendices, are available in an expanded 8.5 x 11 fillable pdf package upon request. Requests should be made using the email address included on the copyright page.

# PART V

# TRANSITION & SUPERCHARGING REFLECTION

## *REFLECTION WRITE-UP*

**Date**_____

_____

_____

_____

_____

_____

_____

_____

_____

_____

_____

_____

_____

_____

_____

_____

_____

## REFLECTION WRITE-UP

## REFLECTION WRITE-UP

_____
_____
_____
_____
_____
_____
_____
_____
_____
_____
_____
_____
_____
_____
_____
_____
_____
_____

# *REFLECTION WRITE-UP*

_____
_____
_____
_____
_____
_____
_____
_____
_____
_____
_____
_____
_____
_____
_____
_____
_____

# PART VI

# APPENDICES

# APPENDIX A

# TRANSITION
# GAME PLAN
# (Template for Copying)

# TRANSITION GAME PLAN

I.  GOAL DETAIL (What, When, Why & How):

A.  **WHAT** I Want to Accomplish (life or career related, or both):

_____

_____

B.  **WHEN** I Want to Accomplish My Goal:

Start Date_____ Completion Date_____

C.  **WHY** I Want to Accomplish My Goal (Most Valued Incentives):

1.  Incentives Relating to My Goal -
Most Valued Incentive #1_____

*Reason:*_____

Most Valued Incentive #2_____

*Reason:*_____

Most Valued Incentive #3_____

*Reason:*_____

2.  Milestone Reward/Recognition (based on date, percentage of completion) -

Date/%/Other:_____ Reward:_____

Date/%/Other:_____ Reward:_____

Date/%/Other:_____ Reward:_____

# TRANSITION GAME PLAN

**D.  HOW I Plan to Accomplish My Goal:**

**How #1 to Accomplish My Goal – by doing what (most important)?**

_____

_____

**How #2 to Accomplish My Goal – by doing what (second most important)?**

_____

_____

**How #3 to Accomplish My Goal – by doing what (third most important)?**

_____

_____

**How #4 to Accomplish My Goal – by doing what (fourth most important)?**

_____

_____

**How #5 to Accomplish My Goal – by doing what (fifth most important)?**

_____

_____

# TRANSITION GAME PLAN

**II. CONGRUENCY ENHANCEMENTS:**
Based on self-exploration, identify three areas of congruency to enhance during the transition.

**Congruency Enhancement #1:** _____

*How to Accomplish – by Doing What?*

_____

_____

_____

_____

**Congruency Enhancement #2:** _____

*How to Accomplish – by Doing What?*

_____

_____

_____

_____

**Congruency Enhancement #3:** _____

*How to Accomplish – by Doing What?*

_____

_____

_____

_____

# TRANSITION GAME PLAN

**III. POSITIVITY:**

Based on self-exploration, identify ten interventions that can help accentuate the positive during the transition.

|  <u>Top Five</u>  |  <u>Additional Five</u>  |
|---|---|
| 1._____ | 1._____ |
| 2._____ | 2._____ |
| 3._____ | 3._____ |
| 4._____ | 4._____ |
| 5._____ | 5._____ |

**IV. ACCOMPLISHMENT JOURNALING:**

___Daily      _____

___Every Other Day  _____

___Twice a Week    _____

___Weekly      _____

**V. COLLABORATION – Thinking, Support, & Accountability Partners:**

| 1._____ | 4._____ |
|---|---|
| 2._____ | 5._____ |
| 3._____ | 6._____ |

Commitment:_____

# APPENDIX B

# ACCOMPLISHMENTS
# JOURNAL ENTRY
# (Template for Copying)

# *Accomplishments Journal Entry*

**Date**_____     **What, How, and Why?**

**1.**_____*(What)*

_____

_____

_____

_____

**2.**_____*(What)*

_____

_____

_____

_____

**3.**_____*(What)*

_____

_____

_____

_____

**4.**_____*(What)*

_____

_____

_____

_____

# APPENDIX C

# POSITIVITY RATIO SNAPSHOT
## SNAPSHOT
## (Template for Copying)

# Positivity Ratio Snapshot

**Date:** _____ **Combined Score for Assessment:** ___ to 1
*(Instructions included in the text)*

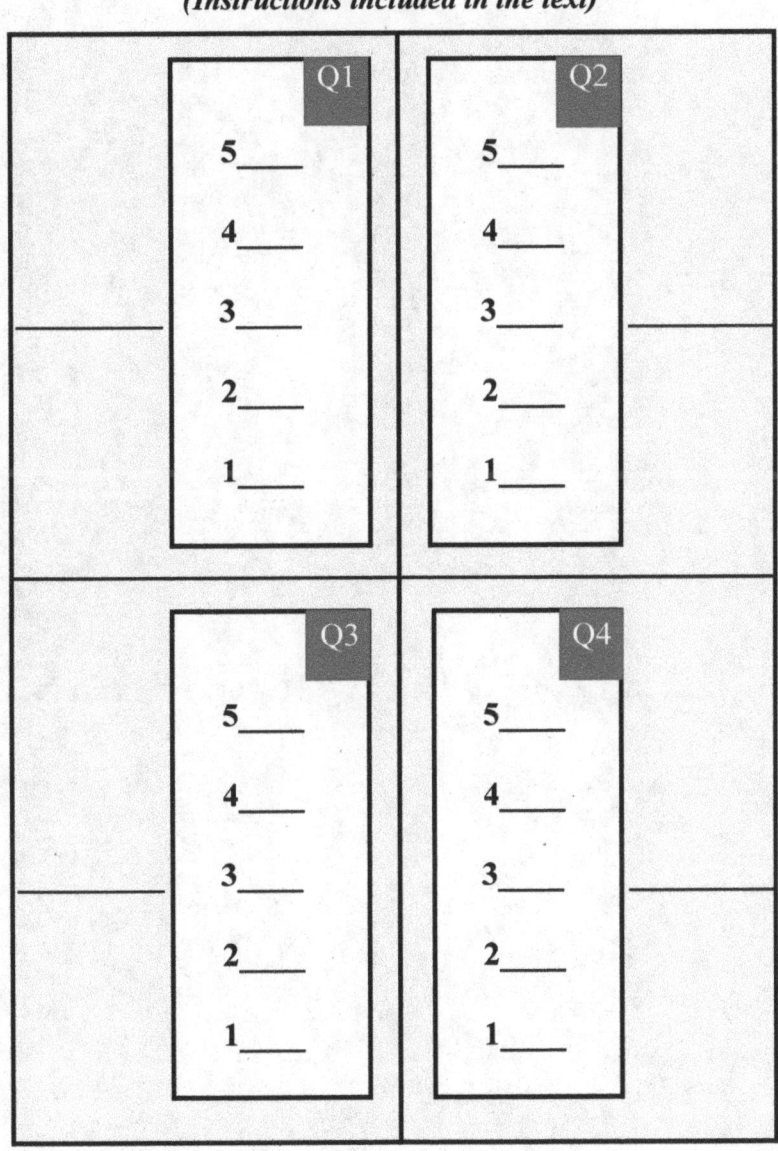

# APPENDIX D

# SELF-EXPLORATION RESOURCES

> **_Important Note:_** *You may find these resources helpful as you engage in self-exploration and discovery. Some of the assessments are free, some have a nominal charge, and there are a few that are more extensive and have a higher cost associated with them. Please note that listing these assessment sources is not an endorsement of any of them but rather a reference to their availability.*

# RESOURCES

1. **Strength Finder 2.0**
   https://www.gallup.com/cliftonstrengths

2. **VIA Character Strengths Survey**
   https://www.viacharacter.org

3. **Self-Assessment Test for Congruence**
   https://www.teacherspayteachers.com/product/psycholo
   gy-congruence-test-q-sort-activity-4685985

4. **Myers-Briggs Type Indicator (MBTI). Must be
   administered by a certified practitioner.**
   https://www.myersbriggs.org/my-mbti-personality-
   type/mbti-basics/

5. **Personality Test**
   https://my-personality-test.com/true-colours

6. **16 Personalities**
   https://www.16personalities.com/free-personality-test

7. **DISC Personality Testing**
   https://discpersonalitytesting.com/free-disc-test/

8. **Career Aptitude Test**
   https://www.123test.com/career-test/

9. **Interest Profiler**
   https://www.mynextmove.org/explore/ip

**10. Careers Search**
https://self-directed-search.com/

**11. Job Crafting (redesign)**
www.jobcrafting.com

# APPENDIX E

# OTHER
# POSITIVE PSYCH
# READS

# POSITIVE PSYCH READS

1. **Flourish**, Martin E.P. Seligman

2. **Give And Take**, Adam Grant

3. **Grit**, Angela Duckworth

4. **Joy Of Work,** Dennis W. Bakke

5. **Make Your Job a Calling**, Bryan J. Dik & Ryan D. Duffy

6. **Mindset**, Carol S. Dweck

7. **Positivity**, Barbara L. Fredrickson

8. **Profit From The Positive**, Margaret Greenberg & Senia Maymin

9. **Purpose And Meaning In The Workplace**, edited by Bryan J. Dik, Zinta S. Byrne, and Michael F. Steger

10. **Strengths Based Leadership**, Tom Rath & Barry Conchie

11. **The 7 Habits Of Highly Effective People**, Stephen R. Covey

12. **The Coaching Habit**, Michael Bungay Stainer

13. **The How Of Happiness**, Sonja Lyubomirsky

14. **Wooden On Leadership**, John Wooden & Steve Jamison

15. **You Can Be Happy No Matter What**, Richard Carlson

# ENDNOTES

## I. Preface

1. Mobil. (2023, December 30). Superchargers vs. turbochargers – How they work? *Mobil*. http://www.mobil.com/en/sap/our-products/why-mobil/driving-performance-and-protection/turbochargers-vs-superchargers-how-they-work

## II. Introduction

1. Merriam-Webster. (2021, August 5). Facilitator. *Merrian-Webster.com Dictionary*. https://www.merriam-webster.com/dictionary/facilitator#h1

## III. Congruency

1. McLeod, S.A. (2014, February 5). Carl Rogers. *Simply Psychology*. https://www.simplypsychology.org/carl-rogers.html
2. American Psychological Association. (2021, August 5). Congruence. *APA Dictionary of Psychology*. https://dictionary.apa.org/congruence
3. Donovan, M. (2021, August 5). *What does congruent mean?* *Congruent Counseling Services*. https://www.congruentcounseling.com/about-us
4. Ramsay, K. (2019, March 29). *Practicing congruence and the art of 'being real.'* Medium. https://www.medium.com/acology/practising-congruence-and-the-art-of-being-real-f597db16cf09

145

## IV. Incentives

1. Merriam-Webster. (2021, August 5). *Incentives. Merriam-Webster.com Dictionary.* https://www.merriam-webster.com/dictionary/incentive

2. American Psychological Association (2021, August 5). Extrinsic motivation. *APA Dictionary of Psychology.* https://dictionary.apa.org/extrinsic-motivation

3. American Psychological Association (2021, August 5). Intrinsic motivation. *APA Dictionary of Psychology.* https://dictionary.apa.org/intrinsic-motivation

4. The Psychology Notes Headquarters. (2021). Incentive theory of motivation. *The Psychology Notes Headquarters.* https://www.psychologynoteshq.com/incentive-theory-of-motivation/

5. Indeed. (2022, June 22). Incentive theory of motivation: Definition and examples. *Indeed Career Guide.* https://www.indeed.com/career-advice/career-development/incentive-theory-of-motivation?sid=inbound-distro-request

6. Farnam Street Media Inc. (2021, September 21). Power of incentives: The hidden forces that shape our behavior. *Farnam.Street.* https://fs.blog/bias-incentives-reinforcement/

7. Munger, C. (2021, September 21*).* The revised psychology of human misjudgment. *Farnam Street.* https://fs.blog/great-talks/psychology-human-misjudgment/

## V. Positivity

1. Compton, W. C. & Hoffman, E. (2013). *Positive psychology: The science of happiness and flourishing* (2nd ed). Wadsworth

2. American Psychological Association. (2021, August 5). Positive psychology. *APA Dictionary of Psychology*. https://dictionary.apa.org/positive-psychology
3. Fredrickson, B. L. (2009). *Positivity*. Three Rivers Press, 32.
4. Ibid., 110.
5. Ibid., 21-24.
6. Ibid., 158.

## VI. Collaboration

1. International Coaching Federation. (2022, March 8). About ICF. *International Coaching Federation*. https://coachingfederation.org/about
2. Reynolds, M. (2020). *Coach the person, not the problem*. Berrett-Koehler Publishers, Inc.

## VII. Summary

1. Encyclopedia Britannica. (2024, February 2). Neuroplasticity. *Encyclopedia Britannica*. https://www.britannica.com/science/neuroplasticity

# ABOUT THE AUTHOR

Phil Schlesinger is the founder of LIFE*and*CAREER INCENTIVES®, a Professional Coaching Company focused on life and career transitions.

Phil holds an M.Ed. (Positive Coaching) from the University of Missouri as well as a Graduate Certificate in Positive Psychology from the same institution. He also holds an MBA from Westminster University in Salt Lake City, Utah, and a bachelor's degree in business and accounting from California State University Dominquez Hills.

He has received a CPC (Certified Professional Coach) designation from the University of Miami. He has also completed a CPCC (Certified Professional Career Coach) program offered by the Professional Association of Resume Writers & Career Coaches.

Phil enjoyed a thirty-five-year corporate career that included companies such as Amazon, Wolters Kluwer, Avalara, and Harry & David. Throughout his career, he has had the opportunity to manage functions and coach others. In the process, he has cultivated an interest in what generates engagement in the workplace, as well as factors that positively or negatively affect our lives and careers.

Phil was born in California and has also lived in Idaho, Oregon, Utah, Washington, and England. He currently resides in Utah with his wife Kathleen of thirty-seven years, and they have four adult children.

* 9 7 9 8 2 1 8 6 2 5 0 9 2 *